PLATO'S ΠΟ

CW00455816

Plato's

ΠΟΛΙΤΕΙΑ

'The Republic'

From Book Ten
The One and the Many

Newly translated by
IRENE NOEL–BAKER

A Eubœa Press Book
THE ALDEBURGH BOOKSHOP
MMIV

Published for
The Eubœa Press by
THE ALDEBURGH BOOKSHOP
42 High Street
Aldeburgh
Suffolk IP15 5AB

ISBN 0 9531004 2 1

British Library Cataloguingin Publication Data
A catalogue record for this book is available
from The British Library

CONTENTS

INTRODUCTION

T RANSLATORS before me have commented on the
fact that 'The Republic' is not an accurate reading
of Πολιτεια, which means civilization, or citizenship.
It is about how to be a good citizen. The conceit that
runs through the dialogue is that the individual soul is
the model for a city; that all the aspects of a city can be
found within a person's soul. It follows that in order
to be able to co-operate with one another we need
to know and value correctly the different forces that
move us from within. People who have overestimated
the political emphasis in Plato's thought may also have
underestimated him as a psychologist, and as a poet.

It is likely that Freud took up Plato's ideas and trans-
formed his three parts of the soul (the reason, the will
and desire), into the super-ego, the ego and the id. Freud
recognised the force of eros, of sex, and made it the
cornerstone of his psychoanalytic theory. Many others
have shied away from Plato's acknowledgement of
eros, and have instead picked up on his advocacy of
reason, thus creating a dualism that has infected western
thought ever since. While the different religious tradi-
tions that followed on from Plato understood him as a
mystic, many thinkers in the Western philosophical
tradition have neglected him both as a mystic and a
poet. Now, in our post-religious and post-Freudian
era, in a time when we are thinking again about how
to be good citizens, when what we value most is freedom
of thought and freedom from dogma, it is time to look at
Plato again.

When I began reading the Politeia I was fascinated by Plato's apparent rejection of Poetry in Book 10, when Socrates decides to expel her from the city, and effectively, from the soul of man. It is difficult to accept, because Plato is himself a poet: if to be a poet is to be self-aware, humorous, ironic, full of imagery and constantly and deliberately using myth and metaphor to draw a picture of an idea (as he says at one point in the Politeia); conscious of the balance and harmony of phrase and word; playing on words and their sounds and meanings.

Shelley, in his *Defence of Poetry*, found that the 'truth and splendour of [Plato's] imagery and the melody of his language is the most intense that it is possible to conceive'. Iris Murdoch described Plato as 'a great artist who was attacking what he saw as bad and dangerous in art.' (*Metaphysics as a Guide to Morals*). Others however have completely missed this aspect of his writing, and have failed to read his metaphors as metaphors, with disastrous results, as for example Karl Popper in *The Open Society and its Enemies*.

Plato has had a pretty bad press since the war from which he has scarcely recovered. I think translators have been so anxious to represent his difficult philosophical concepts that they have sometimes neglected him as a poet; as someone whose meaning is often tied up in the beauty and subtlety of his dramatic and poetic prose, so that missing out on that means missing out on much of the meaning and nuance of his writing.

In my translations I hope to communicate the drama

and poetry of his writing: the frequent sense of confusion and difficulty with which he struggles towards an idea, often with a sense of the absurd, sometimes with a growing excitement and poetic frenzy as he warms to his theme. There are endless little particles in Greek which can be used to give emphasis and act as filler words, slowing things down to give us time to think. At other times the language becomes succinct and pithy, and Plato may use alliteration and extravagant word-play to bring his point home. Always he is aware that his most inspired moments are at the same time his most suspect and worthy of self-mockery. We are carried along by his humour, his sense of irony and the freedom with which he launches into a new subject, or moves on suddenly when he thinks we've had enough. His lightness of touch makes him very appealing to read.

At the point where this extract begins Socrates and Glaucon have been talking about the three parts of the soul, and are now starting a new conversation about poetry. Reading this passage carefully was a great help to me in thinking about some of the riddles in Plato, which is why I have chosen to publish it first. There is the question of why Plato chose to banish the poets when he is one himself. And there is the related question of how Plato can be a poet, and a self-confessed worshipper at the shrine of eros and all things sensual, (beauty in particular), while at the same time insisting on the importance of reason and the temporary, vain, empty nature of all material and transient things.

It becomes apparent that when Plato argues against the existence of poetry he is really arguing against himself, and being deliberately humble in the face of his own skill as a poet, a talker and a thinker. There is no such thing as certain knowledge. The material world around us is our only guide, but it is limited. Plato was a materialist. He communicated his ideas through the world of sense and beauty which he valued, but saw as limited. Central to his thinking is the use of metaphor to help describe things that are felt to be true, but are impossible fully to know. This is the poet in him; he always acknowledges the point at which reason gives up; the point at which we have to call on our imagination to bring out the sense of what we feel to be true.

When Plato talks about art he describes beautifully and simply the limits that are imposed both on language and on art by the inability of human beings to perceive things in their completeness. We all perceive things differently, and none of us is necessarily wrong, but no one of us can see the whole of reality as it actually is from every angle at one time.

As a poet Plato is free, in particular with his wonderful use of metaphor and myth, to embrace a reality that is unfettered by the constraints of time and place. His skill releases him from the very logic that he seems to espouse. Plato understood, as did Wittgenstein, that language is a way towards greater understanding, and that in itself it can only be part of a search for meaning, an attempt to approach the kind of enlightenment that is beyond words.

When Plato lays out an argument he often does so tongue in cheek, provoking us into thinking for ourselves. Just as it is hard to believe that he is advocating measuring and weighing and counting as a recipe for a joyous life (and perhaps Aristotle took his teacher too literally here), so it suddenly dawns on us at the end of this passage that Poetry has won: that the very argument he uses to dissuade us from Poetry has proved the point that she, and it, and therefore he, are all equally unreliable, and therefore perhaps she can stay after all. 'Our words have overpowered us', he says. And we suddenly feel taken in. Just as poetry can use words to deceive and bewitch, so in any argument words can overpower the listener so that she can no longer think for herself. In a sense this is the very point he is making about the unreliable nature of art and of language. It is characteristic of Plato to bring the point home by using an almost imperceptible sleight of hand. One phrase. He can labour a point in one direction for ages and then will suddenly move the whole discussion on to a different plane, having carefully laid the ground before, but without you being fully aware that he has done it. Then he comes to an end and leaves you to sort it out in your own mind.

I think this is why the questioning, dialogue form was so important to Plato. Many people find the interlocutors, in this case Glaucon, to be intensely irritating yes-men. I prefer to read Glaucon as sounding amused and amazed, often making a caustic remark, as if to say that he doesn't necessarily buy all this, but he certainly wouldn't want to stop the great man in mid-flow. Glaucon has to be there to remind us that these intellectual fireworks are all very well, but they can only have any value if they can be communicated clearly to another person. They exist to the extent that they can be accepted in and of the moment.

Socrates was a great talker, and I have tried to imbue the translation with what I hope is the energy and enthusiasm of someone who loves to talk. The line-lengths are to give a truer sense of the breath, the rhythm and the emphasis of the original. Because the sentences are often long and tangled, it helps to present the text in this way, phrase by phrase. Because a great deal of meaning can be concentrated in one phrase, it helps to have the pauses between the phrases, to allow the ideas to sink in. The line endings serve as a form of punctuation, a natural pause in speech while the speaker forms the next phrase. The conversational tone sometimes belies the import of what is being said, so that a balance has to be struck between light-ness of tone and coherence and emphasis. I imagine an intensity which does not fit with measured sen-tences and strictly grammatical pauses. The phrases in Plato might be compact and well-wrought, but they move on from one another like the phrases in music, building to a climax, referring backwards and on.

I've used the feminine pronoun as well as the mascu-line, a style I find very much more agreeable than using one form alone. It is the only licence I have taken with the text (apart from the introduction of the speakers' names at the beginning). I feel sure that

Plato would have indulged me in this; just as I feel certain that he would have welcomed me as an equal citizen if he were alive today. It's a personal thing, because it is hard when working on a beloved text to feel permanently excluded by its pronouns. In the Greek of course there is always a greater sense of the feminine because so many nouns have feminine endings, including the words for soul, and for poetry.

Plato uses a cumulative effect in his writing. He goes back again and again to the same ideas. Once he has reached a defining thought he might leave it and change the subject and alter the tone, as if to say, don't worry if you haven't quite got there, we'll have another go later. Once you are in tune with his ideas, each consecutive passage serves to elaborate and intensify the experience: he is a poet; his writing gives us the space to think for ourselves, and the freedom to make of his words what we will.

This fascicle, if it is well received, will be part of a small series of short extracts from the works of Plato to be published consecutively.

IRENE NOEL BAKER
Hindringham
June 2004

From Book Ten
ΠΟΛΙΤΕΙΑ

The One and the Many

And anyway, Glaucon   595
Numerous things about it
Suggest to me that we've
Most likely set up the city
Correctly

Especially, I would say,
If you take to heart the
Question of poetry.

What about it, Socrates?

Not to accept it at all
So long as it is imitative

595b

At any rate
I think it's
More unnacceptable now
And more clearly apparent

Because we've
Separated out the different
Kinds of qualities
Within the soul

What do you mean?

Between you and me – and
Don't pass it on
To the tragic poets

Or to any other imitative poet –
I think this is all an insult
To the intelligence
Of the kind of people listening
Who may not possess

The antidote
Of seeing things for what they
Truly happen to be.

What good sense do you mean?

I do need to talk about it
But I can't talk

Because I've felt
Such affection and humility towards
Homer
Ever since I was a child.

595c   He has been in my view
To all these
Wonderful tragedians

The first teacher and guide

But we can't
Honour a man
More than the truth

And so I say
I have to speak out!

Of course you must.

Listen then

Or rather give me some answers

Ask on.

Imitation, as a general concept,
Can you tell me what it is?

Because I haven't altogether
Grasped what it's
Trying to be.

Oh. And it's likely
That I'll have grasped it.

Not so silly as all that.
Often it's the duller-sighted
Who see things
Quicker than the sharp-sighted.

That's all very well
But I wouldn't be that willing to

Talk about a thing with you here
Even if it did become clear to me

So do your own looking.

Would you be happy then to let us
Look into it in the usual way?

When there are many of a thing
We tend to posit a kind of thing
And that's how we bestow a name upon it.
D'you follow me?

I follow you.

596

Let's take anything you like there's a lot of

Such as, if you like,

There are plenty of beds and tables

Naturally

But amongst all these objects
There are only

Two notions
One of a bed
One of a table

Yes

And wouldn't you normally say
As to the workman who
Makes each object

That's it's by
Keeping an eye on that notion

That one of them might make
A bed

Another might make
A table

Which we use
And other things like that?

Because none of these workmen
Construct the notion itself
Do they?

Not at all.

But see what would you call   596c
That kind of workman

Which workman?

The one who makes the many things
Out of which each craftsman makes one.

You must mean someone very
Mighty and remarkable.

No, but soon you'll think so.

Because this craftsman
Doesn't only make all the things we use
She also makes whatever
Grows out of the earth
And fabricates every other kind of creature
As well as herself
And added to that,
The earth, the sky, the gods
And everything in heaven and in
Hades under the earth.
She can fabricate the lot.

An utterly amazing genius you mean.

You don't believe me?

And tell me
Is that the bottom line   596d
You don't believe there
Can be such a workman?

Or do you think that
In a certain fashion

There could be a
Poet of all these things

And in another
There couldn't possibly?

And what kind of fashion would that be?

Not a difficult one
On the contrary

Things can be fabricated
Quite quickly and often

Quickest of all
If you fancied taking a mirror
And carrying it with you
About the place.

Soon you'd have made
The sun and everything that's in the sky
Then the earth
Then yourself
Then the other animals, objects, plants
And all the things we've just talked about.

Yes, the appearances,
But they're not really there.

Rightly said
And just what we need
For the argument.

A painter is also one of these craftsmen
I think.
Or isn't he?

Definitely

But I suppose you will say
That he's not really
Making what he makes

And yet that
In a certain fashion
The painter also
Produces a bed
Or not?

Yes, he also, an apparent one.

And what is a carpenter?   597

Weren't you just saying
That she does not produce

The notion
The thing by which we say
What a bed is
She produces a particular bed.

Yes I did say that.

Then if she's not making
The thing that is a bed

She is not making what is
But something that is like it
Not what is.

To say that the perfect thing
Was the carpenter's creation

Or that of any other craftsman
Would be to be to
Take the risk of lying.

Well yes, it would look like that
To people who spend their time
In this kind of chat.

Well let's not be surprised
Then, if in its turn
It turns out faint
Beside the truth.

597*b*   *No*

Would you like to find out
Through these examples
What kind of a person
The mimic is?

If you like

So
We get three of these beds
One existing naturally
Which we could call
I suppose, god-made
Or did someone else make it?

No-one else.

One made by the joiner

Yes

One by the painter. Or not?

OK.

So, painter, joiner, god.
These three are in charge
Of the three types of bed

Yes three

First god,

Either because he didn't want to
Or because of some constraint

From then on
Not to produce

Any more than one bed
Himself
In nature

So made this one only
The one which is bed.

Two of these or more
Were never planted by god
Nor will they spring up.

Why?

Because I think
If he were to make just two

One would again appear
From which they would have

Both taken their shape
And that one

Would be the thing that is bed
But not the other two.

Right.

597d And so I think that
Knowing this

God wanted to be the
Maker of the essential bed
With its own essence

Not any old bed-builder
Of any old bed

And so naturally he
Brought forth this one.

So it seems.

Shall we call him the
Cultivator of this thing
Or something like that?

That would be right
Because it was in nature
That he made this
And everything else.

And what about the joiner?
Is he not the creator of the bed?

Yes.

But the painter
A craftsman and poet of this thing?

Not at all.

So what is he in relation to the bed?

This, I think, would be 597e
The most sensible name to give him:
An imitator of what the others produce.

Good.
So the one who is
Three generations removed
From nature
You call the imitator.

And that's the case for the
Tragic poet

If he is an imitator
He is made to be third

After the king
And after the truth.

I'm afraid so.

So we're agreed about the imitator.
But tell me about the painter – 598
Whether you think that he is engaged in
Copying each thing
As it exists itself in nature
Or is he copying the works of the craftsmen?

The works of the craftsmen.

And is it what they are
Or what they look like?
We still need to make that distinction.

What are you saying?

This:

The bed
If you look at it from the side
Or when you're facing it

Or from wherever
Does it actually change in itself?

Or does it not change at all
But just appear different?

And the same thing for other objects?

Like that.
It appears to be
But is not at all different.

598b   Consider this

Towards what purpose is
Painting engaged in
 In each case?

Is it to copy the thing itself
As it exists

Or the phenomenon
As it appears to be
Is it a copy of an
Apparition
Or of the truth?

Of an apparition.

Imitative art is far from the truth
And that's why, I think,
It can achieve anything
Because it attains
Only to a small part of each thing
And even that is

An image.

Let's say an artist
Draws us a shoemaker
A carpenter
A craftsman

Without having a knowledge
Of any of their skills

Still if they are a good artist and
Draw a carpenter from a distance

598c

They might deceive a child
Into thinking

(Or someone not very discerning)
That it really is a carpenter.

But my friend
Let's be critically aware
About all such things
In this way:

If someone comes along
And tells us
That they've met a man who knows
Everything there is to know about

Craftsmanship
And about all the things
That are known by
Other people separately

And that there isn't anything
This particular man doesn't know
More accurately than anyone else

Then we have to reply
That they're being simple-minded

They've met a joker
A mimic and a trickster
Who deceived them
Who seemed to them to be
All-knowing, because they
Weren't able themselves
To distinguish knowledge
From ignorance and mimicking.

Truly.

Then shouldn't we looking at
The writers of tragedy
And their leader, Homer

Since it's being said
That they know all the arts

All about humanity
Everything to do with good and evil
And the divine?

Because a good poet
If he's going to be able to

Make good poetry
Out of what he's making up

Needs to make
From a position of knowledge

Or else he won't
Make it.

We need to work out whether
People are encountering
Mimics
And are deceived by them

So that when they see their works   *599*
They don't perceive
That these are things
At three removes from reality

And easy to make
Without knowing the truth.

They're producing fantasies
Not real things.

Or is there something in what people say
That good poets
Actually do know about the things

Which to many they appear to be
Speaking about so beautifully?

It should definitely be questioned.

So d'you think that if you had the choice
Of making both

The thing that has been copied
And the image
You'd give yourself up to the study of
How to make images
And set that before you
As the greatest good that this life has to offer?

Certainly not.

But if you were to have a real knowledge
Of these things,
The things you're imitating

Wouldn't you far rather
Busy yourself with the works themselves
Than with their imitation

And try to leave plenty of
Good deeds behind you
As a memorial
And have songs sung about you
Rather than do the singing?

I think so.

There's no comparison
Neither in terms of the
Respect gained,
Nor in usefulness.

So there's no point in asking
The others
Whether it's Homer or whoever else

"Is any of you a doctor
As opposed to a mimic of

Doctor-speak?" Or

"Have you heard of any poet
Either past or present

Who was able to
Bring a person back to health
Like Asclepius did

Or who left behind him
Pupils of medicine,
Like Asclepius did for the
People who came after him?"

Nor is there any point
In asking them about
The other crafts
But let it go –
Only it might be fair to find out
From Homer, who
Does attempt to talk about

The greatest and finest questions of
War, and leadership
And the governance of cities   *599d*
And the education of people

To ask him and to find out

"Dear friend, Homer, if you're not
 At three removes from truth and virtue,

Not the creator of images
Which we decided the mimic to be

But in second place
And in a position to know which

Pursuits make better or worse people
Whether in private life
Or in public life

Then name us a city which has been
Better governed because of you

599e Like Sparta by Lycurgus

And many, by many others
Not only mighty
But insignificant as well

Of these
Which city gives
You the credit for being
A good law-maker,
Or for helping it out?

Italy and Sicily would name Chorondas
We would name Solon.
But who would name you?"

Would he have anyone?

I don't think so. Not even
Homer fanatics could claim such a thing.

600 Can we remember
Any war around Homer's time
That was well fought
Because of the way he led it
Or thanks to his advice?

None

Well.

What about the many and varied
Acts and deeds

Ascribed to people who are ingenious and
Practised in their particular art

Like Thales of Miletus and
Anarcharsis of Scythia?

Nothing like that.

Well ok, if there's nothing public
Is there any way
You could say he'd been a

Guide to people in
The way he lived his private life?

Did they enjoy
Associating with him

Did they hand on down to others
A Homeric way of life?

Like Pythagoras, who was
Particularly loved for that reason
So that his successors
Still, to this day

Strike out amongst their fellows
For living what they call
A Pythagorean way of life.

No, I'm afraid
Not even that is said about him.
Creophylus, perhaps,
The "companion" of Homer

Who is even more absurd
Than his name would imply
As a symbol of culture

If what's said about Homer is true –

Because it's said that he himself
Didn't have any time at all for Homer
When he was alive

600c That's what they say.

But don't you think, Glaucon,
If he'd been able to educate people
And make them better
If he'd had a talent
Not for copying all this stuff
But for really knowing it

That Homer would have made many friends
And been loved and respected by them all?

Meanwhile Protagoras the Abderan
And Prodicus the Cean
And all the many others

Have managed privately
600d To impress upon their contemporaries

That they simply
Wouldn't be able to
Manage their homes or their cities
Properly

Unless these people were
Put in charge of their education;

They became
So deeply beloved for their wisdom
That their followers were practically
Carrying them around on their heads.

Surely those close to Homer –

If he'd really been able
To help people to goodness –

Or Hesiod,

Rather than allowing them
To walk about in rhapsodies

Would have held on to them
As if they were more precious than gold
Insisted
That they stay at home with them

Or, failing that   *600e*
Would have followed them about
Like children
Everywhere they went
Until they'd partaken sufficiently
Of their teaching?

I do agree that you have a point Socrates.

Can we state then
That from Homer onwards
All poets are
Copiers of images of virtue?
And of all the other things that they
Make into poems
And that they don't touch on the truth,

601 But that as we've just been saying
A painter will make us

What looks like a cobbler
To him

Who doesn't understand shoe-making
And to others

Who don't understand it either
But who look at things in terms of their
Colour and shape.

No doubt.

And we could also say that a poet
Who doesn't have the skill
But simply copies things

Colours up the different arts

And laying it on thick
With words and with sayings

So that other like-minded people
Who can only see

In terms of language

601b Will think she's speaking beautifully
When she comes along
Talking about cobbling

Or about strategy or whatever
Using metre and rhythm and harmony.

That's the kind of powerful magic
These attributes exert

But if you strip bare the poets' work
Of musical colouring and
Let the words speak for themselves
Then you'll see what they look like.

I think you've seen them.

Yeah.

I reckon it's like the faces of
People who are in their prime
But not beautiful;

It's what it's like to look at them again
Once the blossom has left them.

Look at it like this:
The maker of images
The mimic let's say

Understands nothing of the essence
But only the phenomenon, no?

Yes

Let's not leave the thing   601c
Half said
But look at it properly.

Go on then.

A painter, let's say
Will draw the reins and the bit

Yes

But they'll be

Made
By the cobbler and the blacksmith?

Naturally.

And does the painter understand
How the reins and the bit should be?

Does the man who makes them?
The cobbler or the blacksmith?

Or is it the one person out of all of them
The horseman alone
Who is the expert at using them?

Yeah, that's very true.

And doesn't that hold true for everything?

What?

For every kind of thing
There are three kinds of art:

The art of using
The art of making
The art of copying.

Yes.

So the value, the beauty
The rightness of each article
Each creature, each task
Lies only in the usefulness for which
Each one of them was made
Or has grown up.

That's it.

So it's very important
That the person who uses
Each thing
Is fully experienced

And becomes as it were
An angel or messenger
To the poet or maker

Telling how well or badly
In practice
The one makes
What the other is using

Just as the flautist will
Pass on a message to the

Flute-maker about flutes
And which suit him best
For his playing

And will order the ones to be made
And the other will comply.

How else could it be done?

In other words
The person with the know-how

Brings the news about
Functional and flawed
Flutes

And the other
In trust

601e

Will do the making.

Yes

So for this artefact
The maker will have
An accurate belief
About its perfection
Or its weakness

Because of spending time
With the person who knows

And having to listen
To the person who knows

But it is the user
Who has the knowledge.

Certainly.

But the imitator
Is it from experience
That he gets his knowledge
About the things he writes

And whether they are
Good and accurate or not?

Or does he form
An accurate opinion
Because of having had to

Spend time with a person who does know?
And be instructed on what to write?

Neither of those.

So the imitator won't know for sure
Nor will she be able to
Assess accurately, whether

Her imitation is
Tending towards excellence
Or shoddiness.

It doesn't look like it.

What an elegant relationship the
Poetic imitator must have
With the wisdom of her creations!

Not very.

But she'll go on imitating anyway

Not knowing about each thing
Whether it's trustworthy
Or shoddy

But knowing perhaps what
Appears right to most people
Even if they know nothing.

That's what she will represent.

What else could she?

So it seems as if we are
More or less agreed
That the mimic

Knows nothing of any real worth
About what she's portraying
And that imitation is a game

Not a study at all.

And those who try to write
Tragic poetry
Whether in epics or iambics
Are all certainly
Mimics.

Definitely.

Well then for heaven's sake
Is this kind of representation
At three removes from the truth?
Or not?

Yes.

And over which bit of a person
Does it hold the power that it does?

Which bit of what are you talking about?

This:

The same thing

Does not appear to be the same size

If we look at it from near at hand
As it does from far away.

That's true.

And the same thing can look
Bent or straight

Depending on whether you look at it
In the water

Or out of it

Or concave or convex
Because of the
Deceptive way we perceive surfaces

And it's clear that there's   *602d*
Any amount of confusion like this
In the soul itself.

So for example the
The art of sketching

Will spare us nothing
When it applies its tricks
To our natural weakness

Nor will the ability to
Amaze

Nor any other such devices.

That's true.

And so measuring and counting
And weighing
Came to light as the
Neatest of our allies in this:

Not to be guided
By what is apparently
Greater or lesser
Or more or heavier

But by what has been
Assessed and measured
And even weighed.

Dead right.

And this would be the job of the
Assessing aspect of the soul.

That it would.

To which often
Having measured and noted something down

As being shorter
Or longer
Or the same as something else

It will at the same time look
As if it's
The opposite in all those ways.

Yes.

Didn't we say that for the same thing
At once to have
Opposing beliefs
About the same things

Was impossible?

We got that right

The part of the soul that follows the measure
Is not the same
As the part that goes against the measure.

Not at all

But the part that puts its faith
In the measure and the counting

Will be the best part of the soul

Why not

The thing that opposes them
Will be the more
Light-weight element in us

Necessarily

This is what I wanted us to agree on
When I said that graphic art
And imitation as a whole

Does its own thing
Performs its own separate task
At some distance from the truth

It gets in touch with
The part of us which is
Furthest from deliberation

603b

And becomes its companion and friend
To no good or healthy purpose

And being light-weight itself
And having intercourse with slightness
What mimetic art gives birth to
Is slight.

So it seems.

So what then?
Is this only for things that are seen

Or is it also for things that are
Listened to

For what we call poetry?

Apparently, for that too.

But don't let's believe only
What seems probable from painting

Let's go on
And get at the

Part of our understanding
That the
Imitative art of poetry
Is flirting with

And see whether that is slight
Or important.

We need to do that.

Let's put it like this:

It is the doing, let's say,
Of deeds by people
Whether freely or by compulsion

That mimetic art imitates.

And in the doing of them
Either they feel they've done well
Or badly.

And about it all they either feel
Regretful
Or they're pleased.
Is it anything but that?

Nothing.

And is a person consistent in her attitude
To all these things?
Or is it the same as with vision,
In that she is at odds with herself

With opposing opinions
About the same thing
At the same time

So that in her actions
She's also at odds with herself
And fighting with herself?

But I've just remembered
We don't have to agree about this now
Because we've already agreed about it all
Quite neatly
In what we've already said:

That our souls
Are full of thousands of such conflicts
All coming at once.

Correct.

Correct. But we forgot something earlier
And it occurs to me
That we might need to go through it now.

What was that?

When a reasonable man
Meets with misfortune
Like the loss of a son
Or of whatever matters most to him,

We would reckon that he might bear it
More easily than another might.

Definitely.

Now let's think about this: is it
Because he doesn't feel the burden of it
Or – since that's impossible –
Is it just because he's more
Moderate in his grief?

That's more likely to be it.

604 Now tell me about this man

Is he more likely to be able to
Fight against his grief and resist it
When he is being watched by people like him
Or when he finds himself alone
In a deserted place?

He'd be very different when he was watched.

Yes.
On his own, I think he would dare to
Cry out in a way he'd be ashamed about
If anyone heard him.

He'd do many things that he'd never
Allow anyone to see him doing.

That's it.

604b It is meaning and custom
That force him to resist

Whereas what drags him back to his misery
Is the feeling itself.

True.

And if there's an opposing pull in a person
About the same thing
We would say that there must be two
In the same man

Yes

And one of them is ready to be
Persuaded by custom,
By what custom dictates?

How?

Custom says that it's surely better
To keep calm in times of mishap
And not to fret

Because it isn't clear what kind of
Good or bad may come of it

Nor does it improve the outcome
For the future if you take it badly.

Nor is anything that's human
Worth such zeal

And anyway

The thing that we need close at hand and
As soon as possible
In these situations

604c

Is the very thing that gets
Blocked by grief.

What thing are you talking about?

Deliberation. About what's happened
As you would upon the
Fall of the dice

Faced with what has
Befallen you

You arrange your affairs
As good sense suggests
Will be for the best

You don't, when you
Fall over
Clutch at the wound like a child
And go on crying

604d Rather you keep trying to
Get the soul used to
Finding a cure
As fast as possible

To pick its suffering self up
And use medicine
To dissolve its lament.

That would be a more
Appropriate offering to
Bring to fate.

So it's fair to say
That the best in us

Wants to follow this kind of logic.

Clearly.

And the thing that leads us to
Go on reliving what happened

And to complaining and
Never getting enough of it

We might call that bit
Illogical and lazy
And close to cowardice?

We might call it that.

Isn't it true that   *604e*
What is vexatious to the spirit
Gives scope for frequent and
Varied imitation

Whereas the sensible and steady way of life
Because it's always
Pretty much of a muchness

Is neither easy to imitate nor
Once imitated, can it be
Readily assimilated

Especially by the people
From all walks of life
Who gather together in the theatre
At a festival.

The representation of that kind of   *605*
Experience

Would come across as foreign to them

It certainly would.

The imitative poet is obviously not
Akin to this part of the soul

Nor does she affix her wisdom to
Pleasing it

If she is concerned about
Appealing to the masses.

She is drawn to a vexed
Changeful disposition
Because it's easy to imitate.

Obviously.

So we'd be alright now
If we took her
And put her down as a
Counterpart to the painter?

She's like him
Because her creations are

Lesser
In the face of the truth
And because she deals with
Another part of the soul
And not the best part
So she's like him in that too.

So in the end we can't
Accept her honestly

605b

In the well-ordered city
We had in mind

Because she agitates and feeds
This bit of the soul until it
Wrecks logic.

Just like in a city
When you put unpleasant people in power
You are betraying the city
And damaging people who have
More to recommend them.

And we could say that it's the same
With the counterfeit poet
Who makes a bad city in
Each individual soul

Flattering the foolish   *605c*
And not distinguishing between
What is greater
And what is less

But holding up the same thing as
Important one minute
Insignificant the next

An image maker setting up images
Which stand a long way
Away from the truth.

A long way.

And we haven't even condemned the
Worst thing about poetry

That she's capable of damaging
The most reasonable people,
With a very few exceptions,
That's the scary thing.

Well it would be, if that's what she does.

Listen and have a think about it
The best of us

When we hear Homer,
Or one of the other tragic
Poets imitating
Some hero or another
In the midst of his misery

Stretching out his complaints in
Endless rhyming or even singing
And beating himself about

Well you know how we like all that
And we get caught up in it
And follow them sympathetically

And make a study of it
And praise the one who's
Most able to put us into
This kind of state
For being a good poet.

I know. How could I not?

But when something at home goes wrong
We make a show
Of doing the opposite

605d

Of staying quiet if we can   *605e*
And keeping strong
Because we think that's manly
And the other thing womanly
The thing we were recommending earlier.

Yes I do know that.

I mean, is it right
For a poet to get the glory

Because we are watching a man doing
What we find embarrassing and
Unworthy in ourselves

And instead of feeling revolted
We enjoy it and heap it with praise?

No, that doesn't seem logical   *606*

But it would, if you think about it.

Would what?

If you remember that
It's the thing that
Struggled to keep control
When disaster struck at home

That was hungry for tears
And ready to be
Absolutely miserable
And full to the brim with it

Because it's in its nature
To want to do that

That's the very thing that is
Gratified and fulfilled by the poets.

But the best in our nature
Because it hasn't been sufficiently
Well-trained in reasoning
Or in good manners

Relaxes the restraint on this kind of
Lamenting, because
It's watching someone else's suffering

And so it doesn't seem shameful,
When another apparently good man
Grieves unrestrainedly,
To applaud and pity him.

In fact he sees it as a bonus,
The pleasure,
And can't contemplate depriving himself of it
By condemning the entire work

There are only a few among them I think
Who can work out the fact that
What we take from others has to be
What we bring home.

After feeding up the pity for others
To a good strength
It's hard to resist suffering
In ourselves.

That's true.

And doesn't the same reasoning apply
To what's funny

That though you yourself would be
Embarrassed to act the fool
Yet when you listen to an impersonation
In a comedy, or even in private
You enjoy it heartily
And don't find that distressing

You do the same thing
That you did with those you pity.

For while you reasonably
Controlled the desire
In yourself, to act the clown,
Because you were afraid to appear a fool
Yet

You let it out there and
Strengthen it up
And without you noticing it
The thing will reach a point where
You have turned into a comedian yourself
In your own life.   *606d*

Indeed.

And the same for desire
And the will
And for feelings both painful and sweet
In the soul, which we say
Follow all our actions

Aren't these things exercised in us
By poetic representation?
It nurtures them and waters them

When it ought to let them dry up

And it sets them up to govern us
When they're the ones
That ought to be governed

So that we can become better
And happier
Not worse and more wretched.

I have nothing to say against that.

So Glaucon, when you come across people who
Praise Homer, saying
This is the poet who educated Greece

And for the conduct and improvement
Of human affairs
He is to be taken up and learned from
And our entire lives organised
According to this poet

You have to be friendly to them
And embrace them warmly
For they do the best they can

And concede the fact that Homer is
The most poetic of poets
And first of the tragedians.

But you must know that
Hymns to the gods
And singing the praises of good men
Only
Will be allowed in the city.
Absolutely true.

Once you admit the sweetened Muse
Either in song, or in verse, then
Pleasure and pain
Will be your rulers in the city

Replacing custom and replacing what is
Generally felt to be
Word usage at its best.

That's it then.
Let's forgive ourselves by   *607b*
Reminding ourselves of the
Facts about poetry

And that we quite reasonably
Sent her away from the city
Because she is as she is.

Our words have overpowered us.

And let's add
So she doesn't detect any
Kind of unyielding

Boorishness in us
That there is an age-old quarrel
Between philosophy and poetry.

As in, "the dog who
Yaps away at her master"

And, "mighty, even amongst
Fools, who idly chatter"   *607c*

And "The tyranny

Of the over-sophisticated crowd"

And "Those who worry about
The finer points
Still have to earn a living"

And many other recognitions
Of an ancient enmity between them.

Let's allow though, that
So far as we're concerned, if

Poetry, whose aim is pleasure,
And if imitation
Do have anything reasonable to say

As to why she should be
Part of a well-ordered city
Then we would be only too happy
To welcome her back
And admit that we are bewitched by her.

607d

Or haven't you ever
Been bewitched by her my friend
Especially when you
Contemplate her through Homer

Very much so.

Shouldn't she be fairly allowed back
If she could give a
Proper account of herself

Either in lyric verse
Or in some other style?

Of course she should.

And I suppose we should
Allow her supporters
Who are not poets, but are
Lovers of poetry
To speak up on her behalf
Without using verse

And tell us
That she's not only a delightful
But also a useful
Addition to civilization
And to human life.
And we'll listen benignly.

Because we would win
If she turns out to be
Not only delightful
But also useful.

How could we not win?

But if not, my dear friend
Then we'd be like lovers
Sometimes
Who find that their love
Isn't good for them

And even though they have to
Force themselves
Still they keep away

That's how we are.
Because of the love engendered in us
For this poetry

Through the nurture
Of fine civilizations

We would be pleased to have her appear
In as good and true a light as possible

But so long as she isn't able to
Make her defence
We'll go on listening to her

And accompany her ourselves
With the words we've just spoken

And this chant
Will make us careful
Not to fall again
Into a love that is
Childish
And everyday.

Let's be aware then
That this kind of poetry
Shouldn't be taken seriously
As having a hold on truth
And being a serious matter

But should be handled carefully
By those who hear it
Fearing for the city within themselves
And taking into account what we've said
About poetry.

Certainly. I agree.

It's a great struggle

Dear friend, Glaucon,

Great. Greater than we think
As to whether we'll turn out

Well, or badly

So it's not worth being
Tempted by money

By power of any kind
Or even by poetry

Into neglecting civilized behaviour
Or anything else that is excellent.

I agree with you
Now that we've talked it through
And so would anyone else.

ACKNOWLEDGEMENTS AND READING

Thanks to Harry Eyres, whose book *The Republic: A Beginner's Guide*, was the thing that led me on to working on this translation; our Plato conversations were the best there are. Also to Garth Fowden, who talked about The One and the Many, and who in doing so gave me a title and made it suddenly clear to me how important this passage is.

I was helped hugely by three editions of The Republic: the Penguin edition translated by H.P.D. Lee, which has a good historical introduction to Plato, the Loeb edition translated by Paul Shorey which has wonderful and inspiring footnotes, and the more recent, excellent and laudably conversational translation by Tom Griffith, published by Cambridge University Press.

The numbering in the margin of my text is the same used in all these editions and is given here for reference.

Printed and bound by
SMITH SETTLE, Otley, LS21 3JP